EXPRESS WORDPRESS

A STEP-BY-STEP GUIDE TO CREATE WEBSITE FROM SCRATCH

Philip Knoll

selves, not affiliated with thi
s document.

ISBN-13:178-1986974264

10:19869742x

Printed in the United States of America

www.itechcrown.com

Graw-Hill Publishing House
2 Penn Plaza,
NY 10121
New York
USA

NOTE

Dedication

To my parents, patty jean, James Knoll and my Loving wife Diana, who is a constan t source of encouragement, l ove, and positive energy.

About the Author

Philip Knoll is CEO of itech crown.com, the publishing company that published several IT books. He worked at Interoute, Europe's largest voice and data network provider. Before Interoute, he was working as a senior network engineer for the Global Internet, a significant Internet, and Telephony Services Provider to the market. He has been working with Linux for more than 10 years putting a strong accent on security for protecting vital data from hackers and ensuring good quality services for internet customers.

Moving to VoIP services he had to focus even more on security as sensitive billing data is most often stored on servers with public IP addresses. He has been studying QoS implementations on Linux to build different types of services for IP customers and also to deliver good quality for them and for VoIP over the public Internet. Philip has also been programming educational software's with Perl, PHP, iPhone and Smarty for over 7 years mostly developing in house management interfaces for IP and VoIP services.

My website is http://www.itechcrown.com

You should check it out and let me know what you think. I keep a blog there for our efficient interaction. I like to invite you to follow my journey, by signing up for my free newsletter. If you subscribed you get a free copy of my books.mp3, pdf files, and tutorials.

The list of my favorite online tools, plus notification of free future kindles book and offers. Pleases, if you're interested signup. http://www.itechcrown.com

Check out other books from the Author

https://www.amazon.com/dp/B07B65WN2Q

EXPRESS WORDPRESS
https://www.amazon.com/dp/B07DYCNW

https://www.amazon.com/dp/B07F41F59Y

https://www.amazon.com/dp/AMNZSJRHSS0I1

Table of Contents

Dedication........Error! Bookmark not defined.

About the Author ...Error! Bookmark not defined.

Check out other books from the Author Error! Bookmark not defined.

CHAPTER ONE... Error! Bookmark not defined.

    INTRODUCTION ...Error! Bookmark not defined.

    THE BEGINNING OF WORDPRESS .... Error! Bookmark not defined.

HOW TO INSTALL WORDPRESS Error! Bookmark not defined.

    WORDPRESS DASHBOARD ... Error! Bookmark not defined.

CHAPTER TWO.. Error! Bookmark not defined.

WORDPRESS SETTINGS .... Error! Bookmark not defined.
Reading setting of the WordPress .... Error! Bookmark not defined.
Permalink setting of the WordPress ..... Error! Bookmark not defined.
CHAPTER THREE Error! Bookmark not defined.
WORDPRESS CATEGORIES .... Error! Bookmark not defined.
CHAPTER-FOUR Error! Bookmark not defined.
POSTS IN WORDPRESS .... Error! Bookmark not defined.
CHAPTER FIVE ... Error! Bookmark not defined.
MEDIA IN WORDPRESS .... Error! Bookmark not defined.
CHAPTER SIX .... Error! Bookmark not defined.
WORDPRESS PAGES .... Error! Bookmark not defined.
CHAPTER SEVEN Error! Bookmark not defined.

WORDPRESS TAGS .... Error! Bookmark not defined.

CHAPTER EIGHT Error! Bookmark not defined.

LINKS IN WORDPRESS .... Error! Bookmark not defined.

CHAPTER NINE.. Error! Bookmark not defined.

COMMENTS IN WORDPRESS Error! Bookmark not defined.

PLUGINS IN WORDPRESS ..... Error! Bookmark not defined.

CHAPTER TEN ... Error! Bookmark not defined.

WORDPRESS USERS .... Error! Bookmark not defined.

CHAPTER ELEVEN .... Error! Bookmark not defined.

Appearance setting .... Error! Bookmark not defined.

CUSTOMIZE THEME .... Error! Bookmark not defined.

BACKGROUND SETTING .... Error! Bookmark not defined.

CHAPTER TWELVE ... Error! Bookmark not defined.

    HOST TRANSFER .. Error! Bookmark not defined.

    BACKUP & RESTORE .... Error! Bookmark not defined.

Preview Of other books' .... Error! Bookmark not defined.

Claim Your Exclusive Free Gift! Error! Bookmark not defined.

Intentionally left blank

CHAPTER ONE

INTRODUCTION

I want to thank you and congratulate you for downloading the book, "EXPRESS WORDPRESS".

This book contains proven steps and strategies on how to set up a website and created a long term branded bus iness asset that will serve you for years to come.

How to use this book

Get your domain name registered, and be ready with your computer and then start. The moment you started in the beginning wit h Wordpress, the book will c arry you along using step-by-step guidance with illustration and simple instr uctions. In this book, you wil l find a number of styles of text that distinguish betw een different kinds of inform ation. Here are some exampl es of these styles, and an exp lanation of their meaning.

There are three styles for text. Text word is shown as follows:

1. Underline text; all titles and very important informa tion are underline e.g. Benef it of using Wordpress

2. Italic bold underline tex t; this is a direct instruction to do in order to complete WordPress actions e.g. click on the Install WordPress button
3. New terms and importa nt words are introduced in a bold-type font. Words that you see on the screen, in menus or dialog boxes, for e xample, appear in our text li ke this: localhost/<your_wor dpress_folder> ".Numbering text or items; the list of item s in the book, we use differen t bullets throughout

THE BEGINNING OF WORDPRESS

WordPress was initially released on 27th May 2003 by Matt Mullenweg and Mike Little. WordPress was announced as open source in October 2009. WordPress is an open source Content Management System (CMS), which allows the users to build dynamic websites and blog. WordPress is the popular blogging system on the web and allows updating, customizing and managing the website from its back-end CMS and components. This book will teach you the basics of WordPress by using the most efficient ways in which you can create websites wit h ease. The book is divided i nto chapters for convenienc e. Each of these chapters contains related topics with screenshots images that exp laining the step by step guid ance for WordPress.

The book has been prepar ed for those who have neithe r the basic knowledge of HTML or CSS and has an urge to develop websites. After completing this book, you will find yourself at a m oderate level of expertise in developing sites or blogs usi ng WordPress.

Basic concepts of Wordp ress

WordPress is an open foundation of the content m anagement system (CMS), w hich allows the users to build vibrant blogs and web sites. Wordpress is the most popular blogging system on the web and allows updatin g, customizing and managin g the website from its back-end CMS and components.

Content Management System (CMS)

The Content Management System (CMS) is software th at can be used to accumulat e all the data such as text, photos, music, documents, etc. and is made available on your blog. It helps in editi ng, publishing, and modifyin g the content of the website.

.

Basic elements you shou ld know about Wordpress

- *Theme System: It allows you to modify or changes the site view and functio nality. It includes images, style sheet, template files, and custom pages.*
- *Media Management: It is the tool for managing th e media files and folder, i n which you can easily m anage, upload, and orga nize the media files on your website.*
- *User Management: the main role of the user ma nager is Authentication, it allows managing the u*

ser information like chan ging the role of the users to (subscriber, contribut or, author, editor, or adm inistrator), create, or del ete the user, change the password, and user information.

- *Extend with Plugins: ther e are different versions of plugins available which provides custom roles an d features according to t he users need.*

- *Search Engine Optimizati on: It provides a number of search engine optimiz ation (SEO) tools which makes on-site SEO simple.*

- *Multilingual: It allows tra nslating the whole docu ments or content into the*

different language chose
n by the user.

- Importers: It allows you
  to import data in the for
  m of posts. It imports cus
  tom files, comments,
  post, tags etc.

The benefit of using WordPress

1. It is an available open
source platform you can use
for free.

2. There are available
different plugins and templa
tes for free.

3. Users can easily customi
ze the various plugins as per
their need to a user.

4. CSS files can also be personalized according to the design as per users need.

5. It is very easy to edit the content as it uses WYSIWYG editor (means What You See Is What You Get).

6. Media files like videos, audios, and images can be easily and quickly uploaded.

7. It offers numerous   SEO tools which make on-site SEO simple.

8. Wordpress customization is easy according to the user's needs.

9. It allows formulating different roles for users, for your website such as admin, author, editor etc.

Problems you might encounter using WordPress

1. It makes the website heavy to load and run when several plugins are being used.

2. The PHP knowledge is required to make modifications or changes in the WordPress website.

3. it is Difficult to Modifying and formatting the graphic images and tables

4. Updating WordPress version leads to loss of data, so it a backup copy of the website is required. The WordPress needed to be updated regularly with your current browser.

HOW TO INSTALL WORD PRESS

System requirements need for installing WordPress, these prerequisite consist of the following.

1. Database: MySQL 5.0+
2. Web Server: include
   - WAMP (Windows)
   - LAMP (Linux)
   - XAMP (Multi platfor m)
   - MAMP (Macintosh)
3. Operating System: you can use cross-platform
4. Browser Support: IE (In ternet Explorer 8+), Firefox, Google Chrome, Safari, Oper a
5. PHP Compatibility: PHP 5.2+

How to install Wordpress?

- *Download the WordPress https//wordpress.org/download/*
- *Create Store Database Wordpress requires*

database MySQL. So it is very important to create a new empty database with user/password. For example user as "root" and password as "root" or else you can select as per your expediency. Then continues with the installation process.

- *Set Up Wizard into your system*

Set Up Wizard is very easy to set up WordPress into your system. The following steps;

Step (1): Extract the downloaded zip file WordPr ess folder and upload it into your web server or localhost .

Step (2): Open your browser and navigate to your WordP ress file path, then you will get the first screen with the Wordpresslogo. In this case, the path is localhost/<your_ wordpress_folder>

Then select your desired language and click on continu e

Step(3): You can outlook the information needed for y our database before proceed ing with WordPress installat ion.

Then click on let's go!!

Step (4): You have to enter the information about the MySQL database as described in the following items.

- *Database Name: Enter the database name as on the screenshot above, you have created in MySQ L database for WordPres s.*
- *Username: then enter the username of your MySQL database*

- *Password: Enter the pass word you had set for MySQL*
- *Database Host: write the hostname entered, which by default it will be local host*
- *Table Prefix: it is used to add any prefix in the data base tables.*

After filling all the required information in sequence, then click on sub mit button

Step(5): WordPress checks the database setting and gives you the confirmation.

Then click on Run the install

Step (6): Enter administrative information needed, It has the following fields :

- *Site Title: Enter the name of the site you want to create in WordPress.*
- *Username: Enter the username you used while logging in WordPress*
- *Password twice: this time enter your password two times so to protect your site.*
- *Your E-mail: enter your recovery E-mail address which can be a great help to recover your password or any updates.*
- *Privacy: this will allows the search engine to inde x your site after checking the checkbox.*

After filling all these information, click on the Install WordPress button

Step (7): After Wordpress installation is successful, you will get a screen display of the stating success by view your username and password detail added in WordPress.

Step (8): After clicking on login, you will get a screen WordPress Admin Panel where you will enter the username and password which you used during installation as in step 6 above.

Then click on login

WORDPRESS DASHBOARD

The WordPress dashboard is the first display will be seen when you log into the administration area of your blog. Thus, it will display the overview of the website. It has a set of different gadget that provide information and an overview of what's happening with your blog. You can modify your blog by using some quick links such as writing a quick draft, and replying to the latest comme nt, etc. The dashboard can be categorized into the follo wing;

The WordPress Dashboard menu
The menu provides navigation icons that includ e some menu options such as posts, media library, page s, comments, appearance options, plugins, users, tools, and settings on the left side.
Dashboard Screen Options
The dashboard contains various types of widgets and checkboxes which can be sh own or hidden on some screens options. It also allow

s you to modify sections on the admin screen.

Welcome
It contains the customize your site button which allows customizing your WordPress theme. The central column gives you some of the functional links, for instance, creating a blog post, you can create a page and view the front end of your website. The Last column contains links to your widgets, menus, settings related to comments and also a link to the First Steps With WordPress front page in the WordPress Codex.

Quick Draft

The Quick Draft is a small post editor which allows wri ting, saving data and publis hing a post from Wordpress admin dashboard. It contain s the title for the draft, some notes about the draft and save it as a Draft.

WordPress News

The WordPress News widget displays the latest news such as the latest software version,new updates, alerts and news regarding the software from the official WordPress blog.

Activity

The Activity widget consists of most up-to-date comments on your blog, recent posts and very recent ly published posts. It allows you to approve, disapprove, reply, edit, or delete a comm ent. It can also allow you to move a comment to a spam folder.

At a Glance
This part gives a generals overview of your blog's post s, number of published posts, pages, and comments. Whenever you these links, you will automatically be taken to the particular screen. It displays the curren t Wordpress version running , along with the currently running theme on the site.

CHAPTER TWO

WORDPRESS SETTINGS

General setting
We study general settings in this chapter. WordPress general setting is used to set the basis for your website. In the setting administration

screen, it is a default setting screen for your blog.

Steps to the general setting of WordPress

The steps to access the general settings are as follows:

Step (1): Click on Settings -> General option in WordPress. Step (2): The General Setting information is displayed in the below screenshot.

The followings are the detail on the general setting page field.

• Site Title: this shows the name of the website in the template header.

• Tagline: this displays a short sentence about your site.

• *WordPress Address (URL):* It is the universal resource locator of your WordPress. It is a directory where your all core application files are present.

• *Site Address (URL):* Enter the site URL which you want your site to display on the computer browser.

• *E-mail Address:* to enter your e-mail address this will help you to recover your password or any blog update.

• *Membership:* you can register an account on your site after you check this checkbox.

• *New User Default Role:* The default role is allows setting for the newly registered members or user.

• Time zone: To sets the time zone based on the particular city you select.

• Date Format: To sets the date format as you need to display on the main site.

• Time Format: To sets the time format as you need to display on the main site.

• Week Starts On: To select the weekday which you prefer to start for WordPress calendar. By default, it is set as for Monday but you can change if you wish.

• Site Language: To sets the language for the WordPress dashboard.

Step(3): After filling all the relevant information about general settings, then click on Save Changes button. It saves all your general setting of information.

Wordpress writing setting

The writing menu setting controls the writing experie nce and provides different options for customizing a WordPress site. These settings can be used to man age the features in the addin g and editing posts, Pages, and Post types, as wel l as the optional functions li ke update services, Remote Publishing, and Post via e-mail.

Steps to access the writing settings Step 1: To change

writing settings, go to Settin gs -> Writing option.

Step(2): The Writing setting information is displa yed in the following fields

• Formatting: This field has two sub-options for best user experience.
1. This option Convert emoticons like :-) and :-P to graphics on display and will turn the text-base emoticons into ant graphic-based emoticons.
2. The second option corre ct invalidly nested XHTML automatically correct any invalid XHTML in the page.

- *Default Post Category: this is a category to be functional to a post and you can leave this as Uncategori zed.*
- *Default Post Format: it is a format used to select any themes for a particular post or select different styles for different types of post.*
- *Post via e-mail: this option will allow your email address to create a post and publishes on your blog throu gh your e-mail.but before you do this, you will need to create a covert e-mail account with a POP3.*
- *Mail Server: this allows reading the e-mails that you may send to WordPress and stores them for retrieval when needed. For this, you*

need to have a POP3 compat ible mail server and it will have URI address eg. Mail.ex ample.com

- *Login Name: login name is used to creates posts, Wor dPress will need its own e-mail account.*

The login name will use th is e-mail address and ensure that you can remember it. You just keep it as a secret s o to prevent spammers getting your link.

- *Password: set a very strong password for the abo ve email*

- *Default Mail Category: this will allows you to select the customs category for all the posts that are being publ* ished via a post by e-mail features.

• *Update Services:* when you publish any new post in your blog, WordPress will automatically notify the site updates services in the box.

Step(3): After filling all the above information, click on Save Changes button to save your information

Reading setting of the WordPress

Reading Setting is used for the set-up the content related to the front page. You can set the number of posts to be displayed on the main front-end page. Steps to access the reading settings

Step(1): Click on Settings ->Reading option in WordPress.

Step (2): The Reading Settings information is displayed in the following screen.

The following are details on the reading setting.

- *Front page displays:* This section is used to display content on the front page in any of the two formats:

I. *Your latest posts:* this shows the latest posts on the front page.

II. *A static page:* It shows the static pages by selecting any one below

- *Front Page:* you can select the actual page you

may like to displays on the front page from the drop-down menu.

- Posts Page: you can select the page from the drop down which post contains.
- Blog pages show at most: you can select this by default, the number of posts to be displayed per page is 10
- Syndication feeds show the most recent: in this, the user can view the number of page posts when they download one of the sites feeds. It is usually set 10 by default.
- For each article in a feed, show: By selecting any of the following formats:

1. *Full text: this displays the completed posts.*
2. *Summary: this displays the summary of the post.*

- *Search Engine Visibility: when you click on the labeled check box, discourage search engines indexing this site, your site will be ignored by the search engine.*

Step (3): After filling all the required information, click on Save Changes button to save your Reading Setting information.

Discussion setting of a WordPress

Discussion setting can be defined as the interface

between you as a blogger and your site visitors. These settings are made only by the admin to have a total control over the posts/pages that come in through users. Steps to access the Discussio n setting

Step(1):Click on Settings -> Discussion option in WordPress.

Step (2): The Discussion settin gs information's is displayed in the following fields.

Default article settings: This contains three more sub-settings. They are:
1. Attempt to inform any blogs linked to from the article: this allows your blog

to send a notification to oth er blogs when you publish n ew articles (pingbacks and t rackbacks).

2. Allow link notifications from other blogs (pingbacks and trackbacks); you may perhaps accept pings from other blogs.

3. Allow people to post comments on new articles: you can disallow or allow other people to write their c omment on your articles using this setting.

Other Comment Setting: T his setting consists of the following options:

- Comment author must fill out a name and his e mail ; when you check this box, it is compulsory for any visitors to fill their name and e-mail address.

- Users must be registered and logged in to commen t; when you check this box, only those registered visitors can allow to leav es comments.
- Automatically close com ments on articles older than days; this box when selected allows you to acc ept comments only for a particular time.
- Enable threaded (nested) comments. When you check out this box, visitors can reply or a dis cussion and get responses promptly.
- Break comments into different pages with top level comments per page

and the page displayed by default; If your pages are getting a lot of comments then you can split them into different pages.

- Comments should be disp layed with the comments at the top of each page;

This allows you to arrange the comments either in asce nding or descending order.

- Email me whenever: This setting also contains two options:

1. Anyone posts a commen t: When you check this box, the author may get an e-mail for every single comme nt that is posted.

2. A comment is held for moderation: This is used in c

ase you do not want your comment to be updated automatically before it's moderated by the admin.

- Before a comment appears: This setting allows you to handle how your posts are controlled, two more settings as followed :

1. the comment must be manually approved; if you check this box, then only approved comments by the admin can be allowed to display on the blog posts.

2. Comment author must have a previously approved comment. This can be checked when you when you

Like to approve a comment of an author whose has com

mented previously and his e-mail corresponds to both posts listed.

- *Comment Moderation: th is contains only a particul ar number of links that are allowed into a partic ular comment.*
- *Comment Blacklist: You can enter your own spam words or phrases which you do not want your visitors to enter into the comments, like URL, e-mail etc.; later it would filter the comments.*
-

Avatars: Avatar is a small p hoto image beside your name. It is like your profile i mage. A three more options where you can set your avat ar for WordPress site.

1. Avatar Display: when you checked it,It displays an avatar beside your name.

2. Maximum rating: You have four other options of avatars you can use. They are G, PG, R, and X. This is the age section where you can select according to t he type of audience you want to display your posts.

3. Default Avatar: In this third option, there are anoth er more types of avatars wit h images; you can keep acco rding to your visitor's e-mail address.

Step (3): Click on Save Changes button to save the changes.

Media setting of the Word Press

Media setting is used to se t the height and width of the images which you're going be displayed on your websit e.

Steps to access the media set

Step (1):Click on Settings->Media option in WordPress. Step(2): The Media Settings d ata is displayed in the followin g fields.

- *Thumbnail size: to set the size of the thumbnail.*
- *Medium size: to set the height and width of medium size images.*
- *Large size: to set width and height of larger images.*

• *Uploading files: If you ch eck this checkbox, the image will be arranged into year and month based folder.*

Step(3):After setting the di mension in pixels.

Click on Save Changes button. It saves your media setting information.

Permalink setting of the WordPress

Permalink is a permanent link to a specific blog post or category. It allows you to set the default permalink struct ure. Are use to add permalin ks to your posts in WordPres s.

Steps to access permalink settings.

Step(1):Click on Settings-> Permalinks option from the left navigation menu.
Step (2): When you click on Permalinks, the following data appears on the screen.

Here are a few settings you can make:

Common settings:

Check any of the radio buttons to select your permalink structure for you r blogs

• Default: it sets your defa ult URL structure in WordPr ess.

• Day and name: it sets your URL structure

according to the date and n ame in your blog posts.

• Month and name: it sets your URL structure accordin g to the month and name in your post.

• Numeric: it sets numbers in the URL structure in your blog post.

• Post name: it sets post name in the URL structure in your blog post.

• Custom Structure: It sets the URL structure of your choice by writing the preferr ed name in the given text box.

• Optional

You can add some custom structure for the main categ ory or tag URL. These are optional, If your textbox is e mpty then default settings is used, With two options.

1. Category Base: To add custom prefix for your category URL.

2. Tag Base: To add a custom prefix to your Tags URL.

Step (3): After doing all the changes, click on Save Changes button to save the permalink settings.

Plugin setting of the WordPress

We study how to set-up plugins in your WordPress site. The plugin allows you to effortlessly modify, customize, or add to WordPress blog or post. The WordPress Plugin is software that can be uploaded to increase the

functionality of your site.
Plugins are used to make your blog work easier. They add services or features to a WordPress blog. Simple step s to add plugins.

Step (1): On the left sideba r on dashboard menu, Click on Plugins -> Installed Plugins

Step (2): The following inform ation appears.

Search installed plugins; you can view your already installed plugins.

Step(3):Click on >Plugins - > Add New menu

Step (4): A list of various plugins displays that are used in WordPress. Here you can directly install plugins from the available list or you can upload it by clicking on Uploa d Plugin.

When you click on Upload Plugin you'll obtain the following information.
  • Click on Browse, it goes back to the page where you can pick plugins from Word Press site.

  • And if you click on Choose File, you can add   files   from your system. Otherwise, you can directly pick the plugin that you need.
  • And then click on Install now. When you clicked on

Install Now, the package sta rts to download and gets installed.

• Then, click on Activate Plugin to active so that plug in to use in WordPress

• After clicking on Activat e Plugin you'll see a message as Plugin activated and you can also find the installed plugin in the list.

• The plugin activated mes sage, you can view others few options such as All, Active, Inactive and Update available.
• When you click on Active you can view all the activate d plugins.

• *When you click on an Inactive option, the plugins which are available but are not activated on your blog gets displayed. You can activ ate this plugin by clicking on Activate.*

• *When you click on Updat e available option, you'll find a list of plugins that must be updated. Click on Update and you get a messa ge as Updated.*

• *Click on Bulk Actions and choose any of the options. Clic k on Apply button to update, delete, activate, or deactivate each of the plugins by checkin g the boxes.*

In Search Installed Plugins , you can type your plugin name in the text box that is already installed on your W ordPress and click on the Search Installed Plugins button

• When you click on the Search installed Plugin butt on you will find some inform ation with your respective plugin.

Step (5): Click on Plugins -> Editor from the sidebar.
Step(6):The following dat a displayed. It allows editing of your plugins. A few optio ns are.

• *Select plugin to edit. This allows you to select a plugin from the drop-down and then edit it.*

• *Documentation. This can allow you to select the tools from the dropdown so that to edit the plugin.*

• *Plugin files. This allows you to select files from the list and edit accordingly.*

Finally, after editing the plugin files, click on Update file.

CHAPTER THREE

WORDPRESS CATEGORIES

I hope you have acquainted with the previous topics in this book. In this chapter, I will discuss how to Add a Categories in your WordPress. The category is used to give sections of your site and group related posts. It sorts the group content into various or several sections. It is a very convenient way to orga nize the blog posts.

How to Add categories in WordPress

To access the Category sec tion follows these steps.

Step (1): Click on Posts -> Categories option in WordPre ss.
Step (2): The Categories infor mation is displayed in the following screen;

• Name: To enter the distincti ve name of categories.
• Slug: it means a word chose n to describe your post. It is specified in the tags URL

- *Parent: category from a d rop down, thimay allow y ou to set the particular category as a sub-category or can keep it as None.*
  - *Description: To add a brief description of your category. It is optional.*

Step (3): After the informa tion about Categories, click on Add New Category button.

Step (4): After clicking on Add New Category, a created categ ory will get displayed on the right side of the page on th e screen below.

A. Edit category

In this part, we will study the simple steps of how to

edit Categories in your WordPress.

Easy steps to edit categories in WordPress.

Step (1): Click on Posts -> Categories in WordPress.

Step (2): You can view Cat egory 1 (Category1 was cre ated in WordPress - Add Category menu). When hove rs on the Categories, then a f ew options get displayed below the Category name.

There are two ways to edit the categories Edit and Qui ck Edit

• Edit: Click on Edit option in the Categories section,

edit any of fields, and then click the Update button. Category fields are the same from the chapter WordPress - Add Category.

• Quick Edit: Click on Quick Edit option in Categories section, Here, you can only edit the Name and Slug of your category and then finally click on Update Category button.

B. Delete category
In this part, we will learn how to delete Categories in your WordPress.
steps to delete categories in WordPress.
Step (1): Click on Posts -> Categories in WordPress

Step (2): You can delete Categ ory1 (Category 1 was created in the WordPress - Add Category). When the cursor hovers on the

Categories, a few options get displayed the Category name. Click on Delete button .

When you click on delete, you will get a pop message asking you for confirmation to delete the particular category, but when you can click on OK button this means to delete the categor y permanently.

C. Arrange category
How to Arrange Categorie s in your WordPress. You ca n't arrange categories direc

tly in WordPress. Therefore, for you to arrange categorie s you will need to install Category Order plugin to ar range the created categorie s in a particular way. Steps to arrange categories in WordPress

Step (1): Click on Posts -> Category Order in your WordPress. The Category Order menu displays after adding the Category Order plugin.

Step (2): In the screen, you can see that the create categories section are not in sequential order.

Step (3): Now, you can rea rrange your categories by dragging the categories as per your choice. Click on Ord *er categories button to save the ordered categories.*

CHAPTER-FOUR

POSTS IN WORDPRESS

In this section, we are going to study how to Add a Posts in WordPress. Posts are also known as articles o r contents and sometimes referred as blogs or blog posts. These are used to popularize your blogs.

ADD POSTS

The following are the simple steps to Add Posts in WordPress.

Step (1): Click on Posts ->Add New in your WordPress.

Step (2): You will see the editor page of the Post in the screen. You can use the WordPress editor to add the actual content of your post.

Following are the fields on the editor page of the Add Posts Page.

- *Post Title: To enter the title of the post, i.e., Post1.*
- *Post Content: To enter th e content of your post.*

Step (3): Click on Publish button to publish your respe ctive post.

Following are other optio ns present in the Publish section.

- *Save Draft: you can save the post as a draft.*
- *Preview: You can preview your post before final publishing.*
- *Move to Trash; To deletes the post.*
- *Status: Change the status of your post means to Pu blish, Pending, or Review er Draft.*

- *Visibility: To change the visibility post to Public, Private or Password protected.*
- *Published: Change the published post date and time.*

EDIT POSTS

How to edit your Posts on WordPress?

Following are the simple steps to Edit Posts in WordPress.

Step (1): Click on Posts -> All Posts in WordPress.

Step (2): To view Post1 (Post1 was created in the above WordPress - Add

Posts). When the cursor hovers on the Post, some few options get displayed below the Post name. There are two ways to edit the Post i.e. Edit and Quick Edit.

- Edit: Click on Edit option in Post1 in the screen.

You can also edit, change the content, or title of the post as per your needs, and then click on the Update button in the screen.

Quick Edit: Click on Quick Edit option in Post1 in your screen.

Here you can edit the Title, Slug, anddate

*of the posts and can also sel
ect the categories for your
post and then click on Updat
e button to confirm post
edits.*

DELETE POSTS

*How to delete posts in you
r WordPress? Following are
the steps to Delete Posts in
WordPress.*

*Step (1): Click on Posts --
> All Post in WordPress.*

*Step (2): To delete a Post1
(Post1 in the previous Word
Press - Add Posts).When the*

cursor hovers on the Post, then a few options get displayed below Post1. Click on Trash option to delete the post.

Step (3): You can view your lists post to confirm if the above post is to be deleted.

PREVIEW POSTS

How to preview your Posts in WordPress? Preview Post is to view the post before it is published to the user. It is safer to preview your post and verify how your post looks on the website. You can edit or change the post *as per your need after previewing it.*

Following are the simple steps to Preview Posts in WordPress.

Step (1): Click on Post --> All Posts in WordPress.

Step (2): You can view Post1 (Post1was created in the earlier WordPress- Add Posts). When the cursor hovers on the Post, then some options get displayed below the Post name. Click on the View option.

Or else view your post editing or adding a post by clicking on the Preview button.

Step (3): You can view your post when you click on View or Preview.

PUBLISH POSTS

Publish post is used to make your post available to all the users, where every user can view that particular post. Publishing a new post in WordPress is a straightforward process.

Following are some steps to Publish Posts in WordPress.

Step (1): Click on Posts ->Add New in WordPress.

Step (2): You will get the editor page of the Post. You can use the WordPress WYSIWYG (what you see is what you get) editor to add the actual content of your post.

Step (3): Click on Publish button to publish your respect ive post.

After clicking on publish, your posts get published for the user to see it.

CHAPTER FIVE

MEDIA IN WORDPRESS
Media Library
Media Library consists of t he images, audios, videos, an

d files that you may upload and add to your content wh en writing a Post or Page. At this moment you can view, a dd, edit or delete any media related objects if not needed.

Steps to go about Media Library.

- Step (1): Click on Media -> Library in WordPress.

Step (2): You can view all l ike images, audios, videos. Click on Add Media button.

Step (3): The Upload New Media page gets displayed. You are going to learn how to Add Media in the next chapter.

Step (4): You can view a bar in the   screen.

The various tabs that appear have the following functions:

• List View: To displays the im ages and videos in a list forma t.

• Grid View: Displays all imag es in the grid format.

• Filter the images and videos: this will filter your images and videos.

• Search Box: this will help s to search a particular ima ge by inserting the name into the box.

Add media
How to Add Media files int o your WordPress.?

WordPress allows you to add, all kind of media files s uch as videos, audios, and images.

Steps to Add Media in WordPress

Step (1): Click on Media --> Add New in WordPress.

Step (2): Then, click on Select Files option to select the files from your local storage.

Step (3): you can add Media files such as images and audios by selecting them and click open

Step (4): You can list of all media files added in the screen.

Insert media

How to insert Media into your WordPress?

Media Can be inserted into your Pages or Posts from libraries, from local storage or URLs.

Steps to Insert Media in WordPress.

Step (1): Click on Posts --> Add New in WordPress.

Step(2): Click on Add Media.

Step (3): You can select the files from the Media Library tab as in the screen below

Information about your selected media file will be displayed on the right side of the screen under the attachme nt details.

Click on Insert Post button , the image will be inserted

into the post. In the attachm ent details field, you will find all the information about th e images such as URL, Title, Caption, Alt Text and Descri ption. You can also insert an image directly from your sys tem by clicking on the Uploa d Files tab. Click on Insert into Post button

Edit media
How to edit a media file in the WordPress?
You can manage and edit all the information about your media that is saved in the Media Library.
Easy steps to Edit Media in WordPress.
Step (1): Click on Media-- > Library and click on the

name of the media item or the edit-link.

Step (2): You can view a list of media files. Select any one ima ge to edit.

Step (3): You can view the edit media page with some few options on the right side.

- *URL: You can read any li nk from the media file.*
- *Title: This displays the name of the media, a title is often shown in galleries and attachment pages if themes or plugins are designed to display on it.*
- *Permalink: Permalink is your URL of the media attac hment page. It is also a link to view the attachment page.*

- *Edit image button: This will allow you to edit the image position, such as rotate counter-clockwise, rotate clockwise, scale, crop, flip vertically, and flip horizontally.*

- *Caption: A brief explanation of the media.*
- *Alternate Text: it is an alternate text for the image, which is used to describe media. Used for availability.*
- *Description: An explanation of your media file.*
- *Delete Permanently: For deleting your media file permanently.*

Step (4): Once you complete editing the required fields, click on the Update button to save the changes made to an image.

CHAPTER SIX

WORDPRESS PAGES

In this part, we study how to create pages in your WordPress.

Add Pages into WordPress.

Adding a page is similar to adding posts in your WordPress. Pages are types of static content and often do not change its displayed information.

Simple steps to add pages in a WordPress.

Step (1): Click on Pages --> Add New
Step (2): You can get the editor page. The editorial page has two tabs, Visual and Text. You can insert text in either of these. Here, we'll study how to insert text into the Visual format.

Following are the details of the fields on editor page of the Add New Page.

- *Title; It is used to write the title of your article, which is later displayed on the page. Permalink shows the potential URL for the page below the title. The URL generates as per the given.*

- *WYSIWYG (What you see is what you get) Editor; It is an editor, which is similar to a Ms word processor interface where you can edit the contents of the whole article. The options present of WYSIWYG editor are:*

- *Bold Button: it is used to bold your text or font.*
- *Italic: Used to italicize your font.*
- *Word Strike: Strikes through your content.*
- *Bullet List: To adds bullets for your content.*
- *Number List: To adds numbers to the list of the content.*
- *Blockquote: Quotes the text.*
- *Horizontal Line: Creates a horizontal line between sentences.*
- *Left Align: Sets the content on the left side of the page.*

• Right, Align: Sets the content to the right side of the page.

• Justify: Justifies the content of the page.

• Add Link: Adds a link to your content. When you click on this button, the follo wing page gets displayed.

1. URL: To enter your URL you want to link.

2. Link text: Insert text you want to enter into the link.

3. Open link in a new window/tab: Open page into the new tab or window. Check the box as required.

4. Link to existing account : Links to an existing content page by selecting the page from the given list. When yo u click on existing page then

you get a link created in the
URL section such as:

  a. Remove Link: To
deletes, the specific link
added for text or content.
  b. Read more tag: To add
read more tag to your page.
  c. Toolbar toggle: by clicki
ng on this you get another
list of a toolbar.

  1. Paragraph: it will allow
you to select your headings
as required for the text from
the drop-down.
  2. Underline: to underline
the sentences.
  3. Justify: to justifies your
contents
  4. Text color: to sets a
color for words or sentences.

5. *Pasteas text: to pastes your text*

6. *Clear formatting: to del ete your selected content.*

7. *Special characters: to in sert special characters needed in your content.*

8. *Increase indent: to increase the indent of your page.*

9. *Decrease indent: to decrease the intent of the page.*

10. *Undo: to restore the most recent editing command.*

11. *Redo: this is an opposit e of undo, restores the most recent editing command.*

Special characters

- *Text Insertion; for writing the content of an article.*
- *Publish; to publish the page to the user on the website.*
- *Page Attribute; Page attributes module will allow you to select parents for your particular page. You will also set the order of the pages.*

1. Parent: It allows you to select the parent page.

2. Order: Sets the order of the page.

Featured Images; includes the images in the pages.

Publish pages

How to publish pages in your WordPress?

The command, "Publish" is used to make the pages avai lable to all users, wherein each user can view that particular page. Publishing a new page in WordPress is an easy process.

Steps to Publish Pages in WordPress.

Step (1): Click on Pages -- > Add New in WordPress.

Step (2): You can find the edit or on thescreen. You can use t he WordPress WYSIWYG editor to add the actual content of your page.

Step (3): Click on Publish button as in the screen. After clicking on publish, *your posts get published for the user to view it*

Edit pages
We will study how to edit pages in your WordPress.
Steps to edit pages
Step (1): Click on Pages --> All Pages in WordPress.

Step (2): You can view About Us (About Us was created in the chapter WordPress - Add Pages). When the cursor hovers on the pages, then some options get displayed below About Us. There are two ways to edit the Post, i.e., Edit and Quick Edit.

1. Edit: Click on Edit option in About Us. You can modify the content or title from the page as per your need and then click on the Update button in the screen.

2. Quick Edit: Click on Quick Edit option in About Us. You can edit the Title, Slug and date of the About Us page and can also select the parent for your page and then click on Update button.

Delete pages

In this section, we will learn how to delete pages in your WordPress.

Steps to Delete pages in WordPress.

Step(1): Click on Pages-> All Pages in WordPress.

Step (2): You can delete the sample page (Sample Page is created by default in WordPress).

When the cursor hovers on the pages, then a few options get displayed below the sample page. Click on Trash option to delete the post. Instead, you can also delete your page directly while editing or adding a page by clicking on the Move to Trash button.

Step (3): To confirm that you have deleted the page, you can view your page list.

CHAPTER SEVEN

WORDPRESS TAGS

The tag is a little informat ion that is attached to the or post for the purpose of ident ification. It tells your visitors what actually the post is ab out. If the tag is stated prop *erly then it helps to find the content of the blog very easily.*

Add Tags
Following are the steps to Add Tags in WordPress.

Step (1): Click on Posts -> Tags in WordPress.
Step (2):The Tags page is displayed, in the following space.

- *Name: to enter the name of tags.*
- *Slug: A word that is selec ted to describe your post. It is specified in the tags URL.*

• *Description: to add a brief description of your tag. It gets displayed when you float on the tag. After filling all the information about Tags, click on Add New Tag button.*

Step (3): The newly create d tags will get displayed on the right side of the page.

Edit Tags

The simple steps to Edit Tags in WordPress are;

Step (1): Click on Posts > Tags in WordPress

Step (2): You can view tag Blogging (How to blog was cr eated in the chapter WordPre ss Add Tags). When the curso r hovers on the Tags, then a few displayed below the Tag name. There are two ways to edit the tags namely, Edit and Quick Edit.

• *Quick Edit: Click on Quick Edit option in the Tags section. Here you can only edit the Name and Slug of the Tags and then click on Update Tag button.*

Delete Tags
Following are the steps to delete tags in WordPress.
Step (1): Click on Posts -> Tags in WordPress.
Step (2): You can delete tag Blogging (How blog around was created in the chapter WordPress - Add Tags), when the cursor hovers on the Tags, then a few options get display ed below the Tags name. Click

on Delete in tags section in the screen below.

   When you click on delete, you will get a pop message asking for confirmation to delete.
You can click on OK button and delete the tag permane ntly.

CHAPTER EIGHT

   LINKS IN WORDPRESS
   The link is a connection fr om one resource to another. Adding links to your pages o r blog posts help you to conn ect to other pages.

Simple steps to Add links in WordPress.

Step (1): Click on Pages -
> All Pages in WordPress.

Step (2): List of pages created in yourWordPress will get disp layed on the screen. Select any of the pages to add links inside it. For instance, we are going to add links in About Us page.

Step(3):choose any of the sentence or word where you would like to add a link. Here, we will add a link to the word Lorem.

Step (4): When you click on the Insert/Edit link symbol then following pop window gets displayed. Following are the fields present in the Insert /edit link.

1. URL: to enter URL you want to link.

2. Link text: to insert text you want to enter into the link.

3. New window/tab: to op en tab or window. Check the box as required.

4. Link to existing account : to add links to an existing content page by selecting the page from the given list. Click on or link to existing account and the list of pages and posts gets displayed. After selecting the meticulo us page or post from the list, the links get created in the URL field then, Click on Add Link.

Step (5): When you float on th e word Lorem then the link

tooltip gets displayed. Click on the Update button to update the changes in your page or post.

Links editing
  Following are the straightfo rward steps to Edit Links in WordPress
    Step (1): Click on Pages -> All Pages

Step (2): You can view the li st of your pages. When the cursor hovers on the About Us page, then a few options get displayed below About Us. Click on edit.
Step (3): Hover on Lorem (Li nk for word created in the chapter WordPress- Add

Links), and click on the penc il symbol to edit the link.

Step (4): You can modify or edit your link by selecting the page from the access list. In this case, we have selected the About Us page. After selecting the specific page or post from the list, then click on the Update button.

Step (5): When you hover on the word Lorem then the link tooltip get displayed, Click on the update button to update the changes in your page or post.

Delete links

We are going to learn how to delete links from WordPress. You can re move the unwanted links which you don't need for your blog or article.

Following are the steps to delete Links in WordPress

Step 1: Click on Pages -> All Pages in WordPress.

Step (2): You can view the list of pages.

When the cursor hovers on the About Us page, then a few opti ons get displayed. Click on the Edit button,

Step (3): choose the word which you linked i.e. Lorem (Li nk for word Lorem was create d in the chapter WordPress - Add Links), and click on the remove Link Symbol in the screen.

Step (4): When you hover on the word Lorem, there will be no tooltip of the presented URL.

CHAPTER NINE

COMMENTS IN WORDPRESS

Add comments; Adding a comment in WordPress allows your visitors to have a discussion with you. When the comments are approved by the admin and then posted to be discussed furth er. Following are the steps to add comments to your blog posts.

Step (1): Click on Pages - > All Pages in WordPress.

Step (2): The list of pages created in your WordPress will get displayed in the scree n. Select any of the pages you want to add comments to then, we are going to add a comment in About Us page. Click on About Us.

Step (3): To add a comment on this page, click on Screen options present at the top right-hand corner.

Step (4): The dropdown list of your screen option gets displa yed. Check the discussion and comment.

Step (5): You can now view the Discussion and Comments box at the bottom of your pag e on the screen.

In the Discussion section, two options present:

1. Allow Comments: it allows visitors to comment on your blog posts and pages.

2. Allows trackbacks and pingbacks on this page: it allows visitors to give pings and trackbacks.

In the Comment part, you can add comments by clicking on Add Comment button.

Step (6): Click on Update button after adding the comment box.

Edit comments

Editing comments in your WordPress can be done only by the admin. Following are the steps to Edit Comments in WordPress.

Step (1): Click on Comments in WordPress.

Step (2): You can view the comments list for the different pages. Select any comment, you want to edit. Click on edit.

Step (3): The edit comment page gets displayed. You can edit the comment and click on Update Button.

After that, you can edit the name, e-mail, URL or the comment from the comment box.

Moderate Comments

Comment moderation in Word Press is a procedure where, w hen visitors comment on posts , is not published directly until and unless you approved it or by the admin, you assign to do so. It manages your comments so that there is no c omment spamming. Steps to moderate comments in WordPress are;

Step(1): Click on Settings -> Discussion in WordPress.

Step (2): The Discussion Setting page gets displayed, with different fields.

In the comment moderation a rea, enter your selected words or URLs you do not want any v isitor to add comments. Whenever a visitor gives any comments it would be moderated by the admin first and then published.

Step (3): Click on Save Changes.

PLUGINS IN WORDPRESS

View Plugins

Viewing Plugins in your W ordPress will help you to enable and disable WordPre ss Plug-in. This adds the exceptional features to an existing website. Plugins extend and enlarge the funct ionality of WordPress. Following are the simple ste ps to View Plugins in WordPress.

Step(1): Click on Plugins --> Installed Plugins in WordPress administrator.

Step (2): You will see the list o f existing plugins on your website. A table of Plugin and Description is displayed.

Names of the plugins; defined in and a brief description about the plugin is Descriptio n column.

- *Toolbar*

Following functions show as Plugin toolbar options on the page:

- *Active:it shows the active plugins on the website.*

- *Inactive: it shows the ins talled but inactive plugins on the website.*

- *Update Available: it shows if a new version is available or asks to update now.*

Install plugins

It is really easy to install plugins in your WordPress.

All WordPress plugins are free to download; the only condition is that a plugin must be in the WordPress directory. Following are the simple steps to Install Plugins in WordPress.

Step (1): Click on Plugins -> Add New in WordPress.

Step (2): Enter your required plugin name in the search box. List of plugins which are relevant to the plugins name will get displayed. Select the required desire to use. Here, we have searched All in one SEO Pack plugin, which happens to be the first plugin, Click on install now button to install the plugin on your website.

Step (3): The plugins automati cally start downloading and in stalling when it is finished. Click on Activate Plugin to activate the plugin on your website, which makes your task much easier using this plugin.

Step (4): Once activated, you will see the installed plugin in the list of plugins in your screen.

Customize plugins
How to customize your plu gins in WordPress without writing any HTML or CSS?

It's usually a large addition for multi-user sites. This latest way allows you to customize your login page by using the WordPres s theme customizer (no any coding skills is required). The simple steps to Customi ze Plugins in WordPress are;

Step (1): Click on Plugins -> Add New.

Step (2): Install and activate the Custom Login Page Custo mizer Plugin.

Step (3): Click on Appearance -> Login Customize section.
Step (4): Click on Start Custo mizing button to proceed further.

Step (5): Now it will launch the built-in WordPress theme customizer. You can customiz e the theme you like and make it look the way you want.

Then click on the new Login Customizer tab in the side pan el. Login customizer page will appear. On the login customiz er page, you can customize your login page in the same way as you customize your WordPress theme.
    Step (6): The customized login page will appear in the following screen.

- *Logo: to upload the logo of your choice to replace the default WordPress logo.*

- *Background: to add a background image or you can choose a background color of your choice.*
- *Form Background: to select form or color for the login form container of your choice.*

Most of the selections in the customizer panel are transparent in nature. You may check all the selections in the customizer to adjust the setting as per the requirement of your login page.

Then click on Save and Publish button.

CHAPTER TEN

WORDPRESS USERS

The function   of   users   in WordPress

Every user has their own duty in your WordPress. Roles are like permissions given to a particular user to have right of entry the Word Press site. These roles can be selected only by the Admin. Here are few pre-defined roles available in WordPress:

- *Administrator: The Administrator has all the rights. An Admin can do anything and everything on the WordPress site such as creating more admins, inviting more users and also removing them. An admin can even lock you out from your site, so it very important to know who will be your WordPress admin.*

- *Editor: The Editor has right to use all the post s, pages, comments, cat egories, tags, and links. They can create, publis h, edit, or delete any posts or pages.*

- *Author: The Author can only write posts, upload pictures, edit, and publish their own content.*

- *Contributor: The Contri butor can only write and edit their posts pending published. They can create their own posts and pages but cannot publish them. They cannot upload images or files* but can observe your site's status. When they want to publish any post, it must be first notified personally to the administrator for review. When the post is approved by the adm in, the contributor cannot make any changes once published

- Follower: The follower can only read and com ment on your blog post s. Followers are the ones who have signed in to your account to receive updates.

- Viewer: The viewers can only view your posts; they cannot edit but can only comment on the posts.

Add users

When users register on your WordPress blog or website, you get an instant e-mail notification, so you always know when new users register, and you can then get into your Dashboar d and edit the users' role. Following are the easy steps to Add Users in WordPress.
Step (1): Click on Users --> Add New in WordPress.
Step (2): You can fill the user detail information on the Add New User page. Fill in all the required fields to proceed further.

•Username (required): Enter the exceptional unique username,

This is going to display on the website.

• E-mail (required): Enter any valid e-mail address. The user receives notifications from the site at this e-mail address.

• First Name: Enter the user's first name.

• Last Name: Enter the user's last name.

• Website: Enter the URL for the user's website.

• Password (required): Enter the password.

• Repeat Password (required): Repeat the same password as the preceding password for authentication.

• Send Password: Send password to the New User

by e-mail check box. When you check this box, the user will receive an e-mail with the new password.

• Role: Select the specific role from the drop-down, i.e., Subscriber, Contributor, Author, Editor, or Administrator.

Click on Add New User button to add a user to your user's list.

Step (3): You can outlook the user list to see whether the users have been added. A message will be displayed as New User Created.

User photo

If want to add user photo in your WordPress, you must install plugin User Photo from WordPress plugins. It *helps you to add your own photo to your WordPress profile. Following are the simple steps to add a User photo.*

Step (1): Click on Settings -> User Photo.

Step (2): The User Photo Options page gets displayed.

Set the dimension for your thumbnails and make the required changes and then click on Update Opti

Step (3): To view the plugin User Photo is activated, go to Users ->Your Profile. In your Profile page, you can see your image section is added. Here you can upload your photo to display a profile image.

EDIT USERS

Edit Users

In this part, we will study how to edit Users in your WordPress? Following are the straightforward steps to Edit Users in WordPress.

Step (1): Click on Users --> All Users.

Step (2): You will see a list of users.

There are two more tabs seen on the toolbar:

1. Administrator: List of administrators will be displayed.

2. Subscriber: List of subsc ribers will be displayed.

When you click on the changing role to box, a dropdown list appears as seen in the preceding screenshot.

- *Subscriber: A person who can manage his profile only.*
- *Contributor: A person who can write and supervise own posts, but he cannot publish them.*
- *Author: A person who can publish and manage his own posts.*
- *Editor: A person who can publish and manage posts, including the posts of other users.*
- *Administrator: A person who has the right to use all the administration*

features within a single
website.

Click on the checkbox of
the username to modify the
role of the user. Then, click
on the change button and
the user's role will be
changed accordingly.

Step(3): Click on Edit option
as shown in the following
screen to edit the user.

Step (4): The Edit User
page appears. Here you can
edit or modify all the fields
as per your need and click
on Update User to save the
changes.

DELETE USERS
In this section, we're going
to learn how to delete users

in your WordPress.

Following are the steps to Delete Users.

Step (1): Click on Users -> All Users.

Step(2):List of Users gets displayed as shown in the following screen below.

Step (3): Select the one you want to delete. And click on Delete.

Step (4): When you click on Delete you get the following option.

Step (5): Select options as required and click on Confirm Deletion. Your user will be deleted permanently.

Step (6): We have another way of deleting users. Here you can select the users to delete, check the boxes and click on Delete from the dropdown list and click on Apply.

Step (7): Once you click on Apply, the users chosen will be deleted.

PERSONAL PROFILE
We're going to study how to create your personal profile in WordPress. Following are the steps to a personal profile.
Step (1): Click on Users->Your Profile from the left navigation bar.

Step (2): When you click on Your profile the following screen will appear.

The following Personal options appear on the screen:

- *Visual editor: While you are adding posts/pages to your site you can enabl e this setting if you wish to create, format, or edit your post. If you disable this setting, you won't be able to use this option.*
- *Admin color scheme: You can change the color of your WordPress site.*
- *Keyboard Shortcuts: If you are too quick at and need keyboard shortcuts then you can check on this box.*

- *Toolbar: If you check this box, you can view the toolbar while using your WordPress.*

Name

1. Username: Enter your username.

2. First Name/ Last Name: Enter your first name and last name.

3. Nickname: Enter nicknames if any.

4. Display name publicly as: Check on the box if you want your name to be displayed publicly.

- *Contact Info*

1. E-mail: Enter your valid e-mail address.

2. Website: Type in your blog address.

- *About yourself*

1. Biographical Info: Some details about your life.

2. New password: Enter a password of your choice.

3. Repeat password: Re-enter the password for authentication. Password must contain 7 characters.

4. Your photo: You can upload an image or your own photo from your computer. This will be your profile picture.

Step (3): After you have updated all the changes, click on Update Profile.

CHAPTER ELEVEN

Appearance setting
In this chapter, we will learn more about theme management. Image files, templates, CSS style sheets, etc. that can help look great. We're going to discusses how to install, add new, or customize themes in your

WordPress. Following are the steps for Theme Management.

Step 1: Select Appearance -
> Themes from the dashboar d.

THEME MANAGEMENT

Step 2: The following screen will appear. Hover over on any theme and click on theme Details.

Step 3: When you click on Theme Detail the following page appears. It consists of details information related to *the theme. Details like version, description, tags etc.*

If you want to add this theme to your page/website then click on Activate, and if you like to just check the theme, then click on Live preview.

If you click on activate then you get a pop-up message as:

Step 4: Click on Customize.

Step 5: On the left side of the page, you can customize your theme. Any changes you make or anything new you add appears on the right side of the page.

CUSTOMIZE THEME

WordPress Customize theme. But now we will learn how to customize themes. Customizing themes help you to give a new look to your website. Here you can modify background images/colors, add titles, and so much more.

Following are the steps to Customize theme.

Step (1): Click on Appearanc e->Customize.
Step (2): The following screen will appear.

As it can be seen, on the left side we have the customi zing section, and on the righ t side, we have the theme you have chosen. So any changes you make on the left side will be displayed on the right side of the page. Here are a few options you must know:

Active theme: you can current theme just by clicking on 'Cha nge'.
When you click on 'Change' you get a list of themes, click on any of the themes, and then click 'Save & Continue'. Then your theme will be saved.

Site Title & Tagline: In this section, you can learn how to add the site title and tagline you want to addto your website.

Add your title name in the 'Site Title' section. And your tagline in the 'Tagline' box.

Colors: You can modify your header text color using this section. As you scroll through the colors you find changes happening on the right side of your page. You can even add a color of your own into the box that is situated in between 'Current color' and 'Default'.

Header Image: you can add a header image either by selecting from the sugges tions or you can add an ima ge of your own by clicking on 'Add new image'.

Widgets: to add widgets to your site from here.

When you click on the arrow mark the following image appears. Here, there are two options:

First is the 'Main Widget Area', when you click on this you get another list of widge ts that are to appear in the footer area.

When you click on any of the widgets a drop-down appears where you can edit more or add more. For instant: If you want to add categories then the following image appears.

In this image, as you can see, you can add your category in the Title' section. Check any of the required boxes. If you do not want to add any, then say 'Remove'. Same goes for other widgets too.

Secondary Widget: Here you should click on 'Add a widget' and you get a sidebar with a list of different widgets. Click on any and it adds up to your widget list.

If you want to add more widgets then click on 'Add a widget' again and you can add as many widgets as you want.

Static Front: you should select either latest posts or static front page for your site.

WIDGET MANAGEMENT

In this section, we are going to study Widget Management. Widgets are small blocks that perform specific functions. These give design and organizational control to your WordPress theme. Some specific features of a widget are:

- *They help you add content and features.*
- *They can be without difficulty dragged and dropped in a widget area.*
- *They vary from theme to theme. They are not the same for every theme.*

Step (1): Click on Appearance --> Widgets.

Step (2): The following screen showing available widgets appear.

The following functions appear on the page:

- *Available Widgets: You can use these to add into your sidebar main menu.*

- *Inactive Sidebar (not used): not used and can be removed permanently from the widget list.*

- *Inactive Widgets: Removes the widgets from sidebar but keep it in the settings.*
- *Sidebar Main: Any widget you add here will appear on your site.*
- *Manage in Customize r: Takes you back to the customization page.*

Step (3): Drag and drop in the Sidebar Main. Any widget you add here will show up on your site.

BACKGROUND SETTING

In this section, we are going to learn about backgr ound images, background colors and background opacity.

Step (1): Click on Appearance -> Background.
Step (2): The following page appears where the Background Image section shows up.

Step (3): There's no image selected for a background. If you want to do so, then click on select Image. You get the following page.

Here you can upload images using two options.
1. *Upload Files*
2. *Media Library*

Step (4): Upload Files: When you click on Upload files the following screen appears.

from your desktop click on Choose Image with the image.

Step (5): Media Library: When you click on Media Library the following page appears.

Select files from the WordPress media library, which means, if you already have images updated then you can select any of them directly.

After selecting an image, on the right side you will get a few options:

- *Edit Image: When you click on this you are taken to another page where you can edit the scale image, dimension s, crop image, and thu mbnail settings, etc. As shown in the following image, make the requir ed changes, click on*

*Save and then click on
Update.*

- *Delete Permanently:*
*If your image off the library
then clicks on this button.*
  - *URL: Enter your image
    URL into this box.*
  - *Title: If you want to make
    any changes in the title of
    the image you can do it
    right here.*
  - *Caption: You can explain
    briefly your image in this
    section.*
  - *Alt text: Give an option
    text to your image so that
    it is easily available for
    the users during a search.*
  - *Description: A little descr
    iption about your image.*

Step (6): Click on Colors->Background click of the same page. Change your background color for that reason. Background Opacity is not used for all themes. Theme customization is not same for every theme we use. It change s from theme to theme.

CHAPTER TWELVE

HOST TRANSFER

We will study how to transfer WordPress to a new hosting platform. Here, we have used Hostinger web hosting to transfer the WordPress site to another host. Follow the straightfor ward steps given below to transfer your WordPress site to another host.

Step (1): Keep the backup of WordPress files and export the database. We will discuss this in detail in the chapter WordPress –Backup & Restore

Step (2): Login to your Control Panel and click on MySQL Databases as shown in the following screen.

Step (3): to create a new database and MySQL user as shown in the following screen. The page has the following fields:

- *MySQL Database Name: Enter your database name.*
- *MySQL Username: Enter your username.*
- *Password: Set password for your database.*
- *Password again: Once again set as previous for authentication. After filling all the fields, Click on Create button.*

Step (4): You can view your created MySQL database, User, and Host as shown in the following screen.

Step (5): Click on + symbol.
Step (6) Click on PHP MyAdmin.

Step (7): Click on Import tab on the phpMyAdmin page.

Step (8): Click on Choose File button to select the backup file from your system and click on the Go button.

Step(9): You can view the tabl es of database uploaded as shown in the following screen below.

Step (10): to upload your WordPress files by using file transfer protocol (FileZilla) as shown on the page Word Press- Backup & Restore in Restoring WordPress Files section.

Step (11): Edit wp config.p hp file as mentioned in the Restoring WordPress Files section in chapter WordPres s – Backup & Restore.

Step (12): Inside the Webs ite section of hostinger, Click on Auto Installer.

Step (13): You can view the uploaded file of the WordPres s. Click on the URL link as shown in the following screen below.

Step (14): You can view the login page of WordPress.

VERSION UPDATE

In this chapter, we will study how to update the version of your WordPress. Here, we will upgrade Word Press to the latest version through the admin panel.

Following are a few simple steps to update the version in WordPress.

Step (1): Click on Please Update Now as shown in the following screen.

You will get notifications in WordPress admin panel when there is a newerversion available for WordPress.

Before updating, it is advised to keep WordPress backup.

Step (2): After clicking on the update link, the following page gets displayed. Click on Update Now button.

Step (3): The following message gets displayed during the update of WordPress.

Note: While updating the version, if you get an error as

Fatal error: Maximum execution time of 30 seconds exceeded in C:\your

WordPress folder\wp-includes\class-http.php on line 1597 then you need to take the following actions:

- *Open your WordPress folder -> wp-includes folder*
- *Open a class-http.php file and add the following line at the beginning: set_time_limit (0);*
- *Save the file.*

Now your WordPress is successfully upgraded.

SPAM PROTECTION

In this section, we will learn how to protect your WordPress blog or website from spam.

Make sure that your WordPre ss script is updated to the latest version. WordPress comes with a preinstalled antispam solution – called Akismet. You can activate Akismet, for which you should have a WordPress API key. You have to register at the official WordPress website. The key will be sent to your mailbox.

Following are the straight steps to follow to enable Akismet Spam Protection plugin for your website or blog.

Step (1): log on to your WordPress admin area --> Plugins --> Installed. The following screen will appear.

Step (2): Click on Activate button as shown in the following screen.

Step (3): The Akismet Click on Activate your Akismet account button as shown in the followi ng screen below.

Step (4): Click on Get your API key as seen in the following screen to get a new key or enter it yourself, if you already have API key.

Step (5): If you don't have API key then, click on GET AN AKISMET API KEY tab to move further.
Step (6): Fill up the required fields and click on sign up button as shown in the followi ng screen.

Step (7): When you complete with the signup process. You will get an API key in your registered e-mail id. Enter API key manually and click on Use this key button as seen in following screen below.

Step (8): If you have entered a correct API key, it will be verified and you will get your confirmation message as reflected in the following screen.

Step (9): Now your blog will be protected from spam by Akismet. You will be able to verify the comments in your blog for spam, as well as man ually mark comments as spam from the blog admin area--> Comments.

You can keep a track of how many spam posts have been stopped by Akismet and you can protect your posts, blogs, comments, etc. Moreover, you can prevent your website from spammers, who can harm your site.

BACKUP & RESTORE

In this section, we will study how to Backup & Restore files and database in your WordPress.

In WordPress, there are many parts of backing up such as:

- WordPress Files Backup
- WordPress Database Backup

- *WordPress Files Restore*

- *WordPress Database Restore*

WordPress Files Backup

To get the backup files of WordPress, you need to inst all FileZilla Client on your system.

Following are the simple steps used for files backup operation in WordPress:

Step (1): Open the FileZilla Client as shown in the follow ing screen below.

Step (2):to enter the Host, Username, Password, and Port-like you have used to log-in to your Control Panel.

After filling all required the fields, click on Quick connect button.

Step (3): You will get all the files and folders of your Word

Press site on the right side as seen in the screen below.

Stet (4): click on the mouse and click on Download. After downloading the WordPress files from cPanel, it will be saved on your system.
WordPress Database Backup Following are the straightforward steps for database backup in WordPress:

Step (1): Type the path http:// localhost/phpmyadmin in your browser. You will get the screen below.

Step (2): Click on the database name 'WordPress' which you have created for WordPress.

Step (3): After clicking on database WordPress, it will open the following page. Click on Export tab.

Step (4): You will get two methods to export the database i.e. Quick and Custom.

Select any one of the methods and click on Go button.

After exporting the database file, it will get saved on your system.

Restoring WordPress Files

Following are the steps used to restore the files in WordPress using FTP:

Step (1): Open the FileZilla Client and log into your site using FTP as shown in the following screen.

Step (2): Open the local directory in FTP and upload

all your WordPress files to your website as shown in the following screen.

Step (3): Then, go to your WordPress folder--> wp-config.php file. Copy and rename the wp-config.php file before editing, in case of a few mistakes you can restore this file back.

Open the wp-config.php file and locate the following code. define('DB_NAME', 'db_name');Replace the db_name with your database name which you have created. define('DB_USER', 'db_user');

Replace the db_user with your username of MySql. define('DB_PASSWORD', 'db_password'); Replace the

db_password with your
password of MySql.

Save your wp-config file
after editing and upload it
to your WordPress site
through FTP.

Restoring WordPress
Database

Following are the simple
steps used to restore the
database in WordPress:

Step (1): Type the path
http://localhost/phpmyadm
in the browser. The
following screen will pop up.

You can create a new database or import your backup in the existing database. Here we'll create a new database name, i.e., new -WordPress and click on Create button.

Step (2): You can view your created database as shown in the following screen. Click on the database name new_wordpress.

Step (3): Click on Import.

Step (4): Click on Select File button to select the backup file from your system. After uploading the SQL file, select format as SQL as shown in the subsequent screen.

Click on Go button.

Step (5): Once you click on Go, you will see a message after the SQL file is uploaded successfully.

WordPressOPTIMIZATION

In this section, we will study how to optimize your website.

Here are a few straightforward tips to optimize your WordPress site.

- Ensure high quality and meaningful content.
- Have the right names for images.
- Use short permalinks that contain keywords.
- Have optimized themes.
- The sitemap should be in XML format.
- Connect posts to social networks.
- Beware of black hat techniques.
- Delete your trash box.
- Keep checking your site statistics.
- Keep checking your plugins.
- Use CSS and JavaScript effectively.

1. Ensure High Quality and Meaningful Content

Any page you create, the most important thing that matters is the rich content. You must have good content with keywords that can be helpful for users, not for the search engines. Content should be comprehensible and not complicated or difficult to read.

2. Have the right names for images

The names you select for your images must be unique; consider choosing images keeping the user in mind. Use keywords that might be helpful for the users. Have some specific names for your images and don't forget to add your alt tags and title tags to your images. For example: If your image is about flower sunda e Ice-cream then does not mention the name as DSC12 346, instead put it as 'Flowe r sundae High street restaur ant-new-york.jpg'. This would be much easier to search.

3. Use short permalinks that contain keywords

The permalinks you use must be understandable. For example:

Use http://www.mywebsite.com /itechcrown/freebook/inste ad or http://www.mywebsit e.com/page-id?5731496325

4. Have optimized themes

Use those themes that are fast and are optimized for WordPress so that when applied to a website, it better not have low speed.

5. The sitemap should be in XML format

Google has several tools that can be useful. Tools like Website Optimizer, Webmaster Central, and Google XML sitemaps are very easy to use. Connect posts to social media

Social media is a very imperative aspect today. So have them connected to you r blog posts, pages, etc., to have good ranks and popula rity. Help promote others *posts and pages too and they will do the same in return.*

6. Beware of black hat techniques

Don't ever try to trick Google as it finds you in no time. Don't put yourself in trouble and create problems for your site by using black hat techniques. Ensure that you use genuine SEO techniques.

7. Delete your trash box

At all times consider clearing your trash for more speed and to have a good flow with your website.

8. Keep checking your site statistics

Size of page matters a lot in your blog. The more imag

es, flash, videos or media related posts on your page, the more it would be slower to load. Yslowi> module plugin is recommended to help you get a faster page browsing.

9. Check plugins

Having several plugins in your WordPress may also be the reason for your page to slow load. So always keep a check on your plugins which you're working on. Consider checking your plugins befor e you add them.

10. Use CSS and JavaScript effectively

Always maintain your CSS at the upper side of the page and JavaScript at the botto m. Allow CSS load first and then JavaScript. Here is a pl ugin that will assist you to get your JavaScript's at the bottom of the page. It is the Footer JavaScript.

RESET PASSWORD

In this section, we will learn how to reset your passwords in WordPress. We have two methods of res etting passwords in WordPr ess:

1. User
2. Lost your password

Let's look at how to set a password through the User section.

Step (1): Login to your WordPress admin panel and click on Users-> All Users from the dashboard.

When you click on edit, the following page appeared.

Now let's look into resetting your password using Lost your password section.

Step (3): In this page, you can type in your new password that must contain not less than 7 characters. Once you are done with setting your new password click on Update Profile.

Step (3.1): When you try logging into your WordPress admin panel, you forget your password and need to reset it, you get the following message on the page.

Step (3.2): Click on Lost your password? The following page appears. Update your e-mail and say Get New Password.

Step(3.3): After you click on that, you get a message saying a Link has been sent to the e-mail address you provided.
Step (3.4): then go to your e-mail, open the (WordPress Site) Password Reset mail, and click on the link that is provided.
Step (3.5): Type your new password, confirm again if required, and then click on Reset Password.

The end

Thank you again for downloading this book!

I hope you've enjoyed this book and we hope that you are going to create a success ful blog. From the setup level of a beginner to monetization.

Finally, if you enjoyed this book, please take the time to share your thoughts and post a review on Amazon. It'd be greatly appreciated!

Thank you and good luck!

http://www.itechcrown.com

Preview Of other books'
The 24 Hours blogging Less
ons'

INTRODUCTION

1 Hour
Once again you are
welcome to most effective
practical guide to the Blogg
ers. The times are allocated
to this chapter is four hours
and divided into the section
that provides background
information to help you
understand the basics of
blogging and shows you
where can sources of
valuable reference material
that will help to achieve
your goal. We also mention
a number of different blog

types, how to select your niche, and list of the many reasons why people like to blog.

Blog and Blogging

A blog shortened as the phrase "weblog" it is a well known as many things that consist of differences digital material such magazine, diary, newscast, collector's meeting place, a showcase for your art, information sharing, teaching hub, the place to learn almost anything you want it to be. A typical blog joint text, images, videos and links to relevant pages and media on the Web. At the same times, Blog readers can leave comments and communicate with the author. In fact, it is space for dialogue and interaction which is a popular part of a blog's success.

In the blogging terms, you would have heard the word

- *Blog means an online journal.*
- *Blogger is the person who owns and contributes to a blog.*
- *Blogging is the act of creating content for the blog).*

You can choose to be any one of the following:

- *Blogger, blogging on a blog.*
- *Blog about a blogger blogging.*
- *Blogging blog about a blogger."*

One of the most important aspects of blogging is that it has made on communicatio n throughout the world better and simples.   Blogs can report any news as it happens, hold mainstream media to higher standards, and provide a specific news and information to meet particular niche interests.

According to Darren Rows, one of the initial and best-known bloggers defines Blog like this:

A blog is a type of website that is usually arranged it contents in chronological order from the most recent 'post' (or entry) at the top of the main page to the older entries towards the bottom.

It has been believed that about 82% of US online consumers trust informatio n and advice from the blog while a small business that gets 126% more leads growth compared to that do not blog.

The most popular types of blogs are many and more to be discovered. The context of this book will only be narrowed to a few of them. There are community blogs, non profit blogs, live webca m blogs, live-gaming screen-cast blogs, device-type blogs, podcast blogs, various video blogs, and many, more others. Few of But most important, and you need to learn the difference between *the blog and a static website.*

We always recommend webbing newbie's and novice to start a blog, in order to learn the basics features of the online presence. But if you are looking to promote your business online maximally (or to start a new one) then it's better to learn how to make a website instead.

Click here to check out the other books

My amazon Authour page

amazon.com/author/philipknoll

24 hours blogging lessons

https://www.amazon.com/
dp/B07B65WN2Q

EXPRESS WORDPRESS

https://www.amazon.com/dp/Bo7DYCNW

https://www.amazon.com/dp/B07F41F59Y

https://www.amazon.com/dp/AMNZSJRHSS0I1

As a token of appreciation, I've included a great, surprise for you

Claim Your Exclusive Free Gift!

For a limited time I've included access to a FREE book! Don't miss your chance to get it, along with exclusive access to more free books and exclusive discounts in the future! Simply follow the link below for instant access:

=>Click HERE to learn more!   <= http://www.itechcrown.com

You should check it out and let me know what you think. I keep a blog there for our efficient interaction. I like to invite you to follow my journey, by signing up for my free newsletter. If you subscribed you get a free copy of my books.mp3, pdf files, and tutorials

The list of my favorite online tools, plus notification of free future kindle book and offers. If you're interested signup.

Thank you

.

www.ingramcontent.com/pod-product-compliance
Lightning Source LLC
LaVergne TN
LVHW042334060326
832902LV00006B/172